To my dad, Mike, for sharing
with me his love of travel and all
things with engines —S. G. M.

To my sister, Krissy, who's never
afraid of an adventure —G. F.

Henry Holt and Company, *Publishers since 1866*
Henry Holt® is a registered trademark of Macmillan Publishing Group, LLC
120 Broadway, New York, NY 10271 • mackids.com

The photographs within the Author's Note appear courtesy of the
National Automotive History Collection, Detroit Public Library.

Library of Congress Cataloging-in-Publication Data
Names: Marsh, Sarah Glenn, author. | Ford, Gilbert, illustrator.
Title: Alice across America : the story of the first women's cross-country road
    trip / Sarah Glenn Marsh ; illustrated by Gilbert Ford.
Other titles: Story of the first women's cross-country road trip
Description: First edition. | New York : Henry Holt and Company, [2019] |
    "Christy Ottaviano Books." | Includes bibliographical references. | Audience: Ages 5–9.
Identifiers: LCCN 2019017998 | ISBN 9781250297020 (hardcover)
Subjects: LCSH: Ramsey, Alice—Travel—United States—Juvenile literature. |
    Women automobile drivers—United States—Biography—Juvenile literature. |
    Automobile travel—United States—History—20th century—Juvenile literature. |
    Overland journeys to the Pacific—Juvenile literature. | Sex role—Juvenile literature.
Classification: LCC E168 .M35 2019 | DDC 917.3—dc23
LC record available at https://lccn.loc.gov/2019017998

Our books may be purchased in bulk for promotional, educational, or business use.
Please contact your local bookseller or the Macmillan Corporate and Premium Sales Department
at (800) 221-7945 ext. 5442 or by email at MacmillanSpecialMarkets@macmillan.com.

First edition, 2020 / Design by Mallory Grigg
The illustrations are digital mixed media with ink and watercolor.
Printed in China by Toppan Leefung Printing Ltd., Dongguan City, Guangdong Province

10 9 8 7 6 5 4 3 2 1

THE STORY OF THE FIRST WOMEN'S
CROSS-COUNTRY ROAD TRIP

ALICE Across AMERICA

SARAH GLENN MARSH

ILLUSTRATED BY
GILBERT FORD

Christy Ottaviano Books

HENRY HOLT AND COMPANY · NEW YORK

When Alice Ramsey was little, she loved to ride horses. Small ones, tall ones—as long as she was going places, Alice was happy.

But as Alice grew up, more people were driving cars. She was curious about the new machines, though she still continued to ride.

Until one day . . .
    when a metal monster spooked Alice's horse!

After that frightening incident, Alice's
husband, John, had an idea to keep her safe.
John believed that cars were more reliable
than horses. They didn't get scared.

From the moment Alice slid behind the driver's wheel, she was in love. She even entered a two-day endurance run to test her driving skills. She earned a perfect score and wowed a fellow driver who worked for Maxwell-Briscoe, the makers of Alice's car.

At dinner after the first day's run, her fellow driver, the carmaker's publicist, had a proposal for Alice. He asked if she would drive from New York to California in a new Maxwell car to show the world that the cars were so well built and easy to operate that even a *lady* could drive one safely. He didn't think women were as good at doing things as men, and he wasn't the only one.

The trip sounded challenging, partly because so many roads on the route were unpaved. Also, while the Maxwell company would offer help to Alice in the form of a guide car in most states, she might sometimes need to rely on her own repair skills to keep the car running.

Still, Alice was intrigued. She was about to show the Maxwell publicist—and the world—that ladies could drive just as well as men. Maybe even better.

She told him she'd do it. And that she'd be bringing some friends.

ALICE PREPARES FOR HER DRIVE

As the Maxwell company ran notices about the trip in newspapers across the country, Alice continued to hone her skills, like cleaning spark plugs and changing tires. The more she could do on her own, the better prepared she'd be.

Nine months later, on a rainy June morning in New York City, Alice and her three friends started their journey.

Alice's friend Hermine eagerly looked toward the western horizon, where California was waiting. Alice's sisters-in-law Nettie and Maggie shivered as Alice cranked the car to start it.

Armed with a camera, guidebooks, maps, and some emergency
food rations, they were as ready as they'd ever be.

On this day, driving might have felt different to Alice—perhaps a little scary,
like the first time she'd ridden a horse. Still, she had skills and knowledge that
she was eager to put to the test, and this was the perfect opportunity.

As the car rumbled down the rain-soaked road, picking up speed, Alice's nerves disappeared. Hermine even asked if Alice would give her driving lessons when they got home.

Over the next several days,
they blazed through Cleveland and
soared toward Chicago.
Nothing could slow them down, except . . .

Bump!
Rattle!
BANG!

They got their first flat tire, and they hadn't even reached Toledo yet.
Once Alice made repairs, they journeyed to Chicago, where the car was hit in a traffic jam. No one was hurt, though a hubcap was dented. They stayed in the city for three days before continuing to blaze a trail westward, hoping for miles of blue sky.

But as the days went on and they crossed west of the
Mississippi River, the skies over Iowa became dark. The car
wheezed and stalled, overheated from a hard day's travel.

Hermine sighed. They were stuck. But Alice knew what they
needed: water to cool the radiator.

Nettie and Maggie exchanged a look. The well-to-do sisters
grabbed their cut-glass toiletry jars and carefully scooped up
water, ounce by ounce, from a nearby ditch.

Alice's friends were helping her on the journey without ever
taking the wheel!

As they drove on, heavy rains turned the dirt roads into a muddy mess. Worse, the river in their path had risen too high to cross, forcing them to wait for the rain to let up and the river to recede. With no town in sight, they would have to camp in the car.

When they were finally ready to set off again, the mud had other ideas. Farmers had to be fetched from a nearby farmhouse to help tow the car to safety.

At last, they were back on the road.

Soon people began waiting by the roadside to catch a glimpse of the women who changed flat tires, repaired broken brake pedals, and cleaned spark plugs. Some folks didn't believe Alice and her team would ever reach California. But others were excited and showed up to cheer the women on their way.

Sometimes Alice gave interviews to local newspapers.
But her mind was elsewhere, focused on their maps and
directions to ensure they stayed on course.

Alice found herself driving faster through the Midwest,
hoping they'd reach a town soon, when . . .

. . . they landed in a pothole more stubborn than Alice herself!
They would have to fix this quickly. It was nearly dark.

Alice started to have doubts.
There had been people along the journey who
disapproved of her being a woman and wanting to drive.
There were still those who thought she wouldn't make it.

The only way to silence everyone's doubts,
including her own, was to reach California, no
matter how many potholes stood in the way.

Alice had to keep going. She *could* keep going. She'd gotten them this far, after all, driving for more than a month to reach a part of the country she'd never seen.

With some quick thinking, she could cross
any distance, solve any problem.

As they sped west, Alice followed the trails of old wagon
tracks, which led them through a Nebraska town where the
road was blocked by a sheriff and his men searching for an
escaped criminal! It took nearly two hours to catch
him before the women were able to move on.

The next day they were back on the road and headed to Wyoming. Their directions here were sometimes unclear, so Alice began following the wires of telegraph poles, trusting them to lead her toward towns.

Two days after entering the state, Alice was exhausted, having crossed the North Platte River on a railroad bridge.

Luckily, Hermine spotted a roadside hotel.

But it turned out the hotel's beds were already occupied . . .

by bedbugs!

Back on the road, Alice pressed the gas. California was on the horizon.

Of course, things still weren't easy. Sometimes they hit dead ends, forcing them to backtrack for miles through stifling heat. And sometimes there was little more to eat than corn flakes and canned tomatoes scrounged from a general store.

But nothing—not hunger, hot days, chilly rain, washed-out roads, or the worst mud—could stop Alice now.

One day, as they drove into
view of towering mountain
slopes where ancient sequoia
trees stood tall and proud,
Alice's stomach flipped.

The looming Sierra Nevada
Mountains and their strange
trees could mean only one thing:
California!

They had done it!

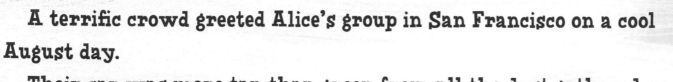

A terrific crowd greeted Alice's group in San Francisco on a cool August day.

Their car was more tan than green from all the dust gathered on its two-month, nearly four-thousand-mile journey.

Alice waved to the many strangers, who weren't laughing but cheering as she drove in a motorcade with horns blaring in celebration.

Now the world understood: A lady could drive just as well as a man. Or even better.

Over miles and miles of unpaved roads, through rough weather conditions, brave Alice had become guide, mechanic, and leader of her group—and the first female driver to successfully cross the country.

AUTHOR'S NOTE
The Life and Legacy of Alice Ramsey

Alice Huyler Ramsey (November 11, 1886–September 10, 1983) was one of the first prominent female drivers, the first woman to complete a cross-country American road trip, and the first woman to earn a place in the Automotive Hall of Fame. She grew up in Hackensack, New Jersey, and attended Vassar College from 1903 to 1905, after which she married John Ramsey and had a son.

Only a year after she first slid behind the wheel, the twenty-two-year-old housewife and mother embarked on a drive across America on June 9, 1909, to help the Maxwell-Briscoe Company promote its cars—a journey no women (and only a few men) had ever driven. At a time when women couldn't vote and were expected to keep out of traditional male roles, Alice would not stay home. After all, she had already driven in and won an endurance race against many male competitors, while her husband didn't even know how to drive!

Alice sits behind the wheel.

There were many hardships in Alice's path from New York to California, not least of which were the physical demands of such a journey. The car's crank-start handle was heavy and hard to turn, yet Alice had to do so multiple times a day. The car's retractable roof, roll-up windshield, and open-side design also meant she was often exposed to the elements—heat, cold, dust, and plenty of wind and rain. The Maxwell company hired a newsman, J. D. Murphy, to precede the women by train and arrange for food and lodging—and, of course, to do interviews. The company also provided local escorts, replacement parts, and mechanics for the larger repairs. But it was up to Alice to plan her driving route and deal with whatever challenges came up. From Alice's resourcefulness in using telegraph wires to guide her from town to town, to her self-taught skills as a mechanic so that she

Alice changes a tire.

could handle many of the car's breakdowns on her own, Alice steadily blazed a trail for other women to follow as she fearlessly drove toward California.

After Alice's successful trip, which wound up taking a total of 59 days over 3,800 miles of road (only approximately 152 miles of which were paved), the Maxwell-Briscoe Company—eventually absorbed as part of Chrysler Group—started calling its Maxwell DA "the car for a lady to drive."

Though Alice and her friends attracted crowds of admirers and had the support of the Maxwell-Briscoe Company, their journey was also met with disapproval. Some newspapers of the early 1900s called the trip "ridiculous." Others said the drive was "beyond the capabilities of women

The foursome drove over 3,800 miles from New York to California.

Alice Ramsey and her three driving companions. From left to right: Hermine Jahns, Margaret Atwood, Nettie Powell, and Alice Ramsey.

drivers." In her 1961 memoir, *Veil, Duster, and Tire Iron*, which gives a rich account of her journey, Alice said, "This criticism, of course, merely whetted the appetites of those of us who were convinced that we could drive as well as most men. . . . It's been done by men and as long as they have been able to accomplish it, why shouldn't I?"

Although Alice's accomplishment largely faded from public memory, the landscape for American drivers changed drastically over time. Alice paved the way for female drivers by reaching the finish line in California. After that historic 1909 trip, she continued to do what she loved best: cruise the open road. She made at least thirty more cross-country drives, and in all that time, only ever received one ticket—in California, for making an illegal U-turn—but she didn't let that keep her off the road for long.

From left to right: Hermine, Alice, Margaret, and Nettie pose for cameras on their cross-country tour.

THE MAIN STREET OF AMERICA
A Note on Cars from Alice's Time to Today

Cars have been around for a long time—longer than you might think. As far back as the 1770s, people were trying to invent ways to get from one place to another in record time. In 1885, a German inventor named Karl Benz created the first gas-powered motorcar. These cars reached a top speed of 10 miles per hour. That may seem slow, but back then, it was a big deal. Karl Benz's wife, Bertha, was also a big deal: In 1888, she took one of the cars for a 66-mile drive, becoming the first person to take a long-distance automobile trip. While on the drive, she invented brake lining, improving the safety of cars—something Alice Ramsey would value twenty years later.

Soon, gas-powered cars became more common in America. In 1908, just one year before Alice's big drive, Henry Ford introduced the Model T, a mass-produced car intended for ordinary families. Expensive at first, the Model T's price dropped by more than half in the next ten years with Ford's innovations in assembly line production. By the end of its run in 1927, more than fifteen million Model T's had rolled out of Ford factories.

As cars became widely produced and affordable for families, the need for paved roads became evident. A huge network of paved roads known as Route 66 was perhaps the most famous U.S. highway. Designed in 1926, this route was 2,448 miles long, stretching from Chicago to Los Angeles through eight states: Illinois, Missouri, Kansas, Oklahoma, Texas, New Mexico, Arizona, and California. Route 66 made it easier for people from one city or town to travel to another and for companies to send goods from one place to the next.

In the early 1930s, thousands of people would use Route 66 to flee the severe drought of the Dust Bowl, a long and frightening period of dust storms across parts of the Midwest. The route became known by many affectionate names, like "The Mother Road" and "The Main Street of America."

With America's economic prosperity after World War II, businesses like diners, gas stations, motels, and even tourist attractions sprang up along the route. Its roads were flat and easily accessible, and among the route's many attractions was the first-ever McDonald's.

Shortly after the war, Route 66 was displaced by something even bigger: the Interstate Highway System. President Dwight D. Eisenhower was inspired to create this larger, more efficient highway system when he was fighting in the war in Germany. Their huge network of high-speed roads allowed the military to travel quickly, and he wanted to bring that same mobility to America. The wide, limited-access expressways would bypass local towns to avoid congestion, making it easier to get out of cities in case of emergency, and making coast-to-coast travel much quicker.

Cars and the highway system meant Americans who owned vehicles could travel more, walk less, and live farther away from their jobs, shaping the suburbs that many of us live in. Alice was part of a movement that greatly changed the structure and culture of America, helping to make it the place we know today.

SELECTED BIBLIOGRAPHY

Jensen, Cheryl. "American Women at the Wheel; By Blazing a Coast-to-Coast Trail, She Helped Put a Nation on the Road." *The New York Times*. June 6, 1999.

Kay, Jane Holtz. *Asphalt Nation: How the Automobile Took Over America and How We Can Take It Back*. Berkeley: University of California Press, 1997.

McConnell, Curt. "*A Reliable Car and a Woman Who Knows It*": The First Coast-to-Coast Auto Trips by Women, 1899–1916. Jefferson, NC: McFarland, 2000.

Ramsey, Alice Huyler. *Veil, Duster, and Tire Iron*. Covina, CA: Castle Press, 1961.

Ruben, Marina Koestler. "Alice Ramsey's Historic Cross-Country Drive." Smithsonian.com, June 4, 2009. smithsonianmag.com/history/alice-ramseys-historic-cross-country-drive-29114570/.

Vassar College Special Collections: Alice Huyler Ramsey Papers. specialcollections.vassar.edu /collections/manuscripts/findingaids/ramsey_alice_huyler.html.